YOUR KNOWLEDGE H

- We will publish your bachelor's and
  master's thesis, essays and papers

- Your own eBook and book -
  sold worldwide in all relevant shops

- Earn money with each sale

Upload your text at www.GRIN.com
and publish for free

Junaid Javaid

Virtual Teams & Project Management

GRIN Verlag

Bibliografische Information der Deutschen Nationalbibliothek:

Die Deutsche Bibliothek verzeichnet diese Publikation in der Deutschen National-
bibliografie; detaillierte bibliografische Daten sind im Internet über http://dnb.d-
nb.de/ abrufbar.

Imprint:

Copyright © 2014 GRIN Verlag GmbH
Druck und Bindung: Books on Demand GmbH, Norderstedt Germany
ISBN: 978-3-656-74814-4

This book at GRIN:

http://www.grin.com/en/e-book/280881/virtual-teams-project-management

GRIN - Your knowledge has value

Der GRIN Verlag publiziert seit 1998 wissenschaftliche Arbeiten von Studenten, Hochschullehrern und anderen Akademikern als eBook und gedrucktes Buch. Die Verlagswebsite www.grin.com ist die ideale Plattform zur Veröffentlichung von Hausarbeiten, Abschlussarbeiten, wissenschaftlichen Aufsätzen, Dissertationen und Fachbüchern.

Visit us on the internet:

http://www.grin.com/

http://www.facebook.com/grincom

http://www.twitter.com/grin_com

PM1- VIRTUAL TEAMS & PROJECT MANAGEMENT

ASSESSMENT-2: APPLIED MANAGEMENT PROJECT

WRITTEN & SUBMITTED BY:

JUNAID JAVAID

COURSE NAME:

MSc PROJECT MANAGEMENT

UNIT NAME:

BUSINESS RESEARCH METHODS

DATE OF SUBMISSION:

28-APRIL-2014

Table of Contents

Executive Summary

This Applied Management Project (AMP) is written on the topic of Cultural Diversity Issue and its Implications on the Communication over Global Virtual Team (GVT) members. The scope of this report is broad as it will not only outline major challenges faced by virtual teams because of aspect of cultural differences but also investigate that how this challenge could make influence on the effectiveness of GVT. It has been discovered that Global Virtual Team is determined as a collaboration of individuals where each group member interacts through interdependent tasks directed by the common objective and this team works across links that are strengthened through several aspects (communication, information and multimedia technologies). It has been learned from previous case studies on GVT that cultural difference could have positive impact on knowledge sharing as the component of intercultural encounter intends to make tacit and contextual knowledge as explicit. It has been contended that the factor of cultural diversity is useful in developing trust between all involved members. In regard to cross-cultural communication theories, the model proposed by Hofstede (1996) always ranked at the top. This framework is very useful in directing individuals that how should one could distinguish among the characteristics of each other cultures. It has been analysed that there are various challenges (Communication Challenge, Accent & Fluency Challenge, Attitude Challenge, Decision Making Challenge, Lack of Awareness, Inability in Building Social Bonds, Lack of Trust and Lack of Agreement) that could be faced by GVT. In short, it has been predicted that all of these cultural challenges being faced by GVT would impede virtual teams' capabilities in accomplishing their tasks and projects. From the case study on BakBone Software Inc., It has been observed that despite of certain cross-cultural communication and cultural differences issues BakBone Software Inc. has managed to perform well. And the company attribute such success to the fact that all of team members have interaction with each other on continuous basis. And this has intended them to remain informed about each other strengths and thus results in developing and maintaining great extent of trust. It has been recommended that the company's managers need to be aware all cultural issues that could cause problem to the communication aspect within Global Virtual Teams.

Chapter-1: Background Context with Aims & Objectives

1.1. Background Context

This Applied Management Project (AMP) is written on the topic of Cultural Diversity Issue and its Implications on the Communication over Global Virtual Team (GVT) members. The scope of this report is broad as it will not only outline major challenges faced by virtual teams because of aspect of cultural differences but also investigate that how this challenge could make influence on the effectiveness of GVT. It has been discovered that there are large number research studies conducted on the topic for the purpose of investigating cultural issues within virtual teams (Suchan & Greg, 2001; Young, 2001). A virtual team is also known as multi-cultural team because of the fact that very often the members involved in these forms of teams have different cultural backgrounds as they are from different countries (Vinaja, 2004). Therefore, it has been analysed that within the context of global marketplace, more and more companies are in a need of having international presence and hence this phenomenon has created the demands for virtual teams (Rosenhauer, 2008). There are many that Companies have adopted the approach of allocating individuals to projects on the basis of their expertise. And this approach has made possible for these companies to assign tasks and appropriate project to competent and qualified people without having to expose themselves towards wasted productivity problems that usually caused due to frequent relocation or extensive travel (Goldman, 2000).

In general, the concept of Multi-Cultural virtual teams is seems to be significant in the current era of corporate specifically due to two major reasons: the proliferation of network technologies in the shapes of Information Systems (IS) and the increasing globalisation of organisations (Moodian, 2007). However there are certain problems (lack of synergies, communication breakdowns, time delays in replies, different holiday periods and working hours) that have been experienced by companies within multi-cultural virtual teams. It has been discovered that the multi-cultural issues within the virtual teams are not always evident (visible) but surely it exists (Lustig & Koester, 2009). According to various studies on Virtual Teams, it has been outlined that Global Virtual Teams (GVT) in the most cases are subject to important challenges within the four main areas: cultural diversity, communication, technology and language (Kayworth & Dorthy, 2000). Additionally, it has been identified that all of these challenges could make negative influence on four major factors: Trust, Control, Motivation and Communication and all of these aspects are collectively significant for the determination of GVT effectiveness (Tomovic, 2011).

It has been observed that the researchers are in the pursuit of finding out that how the cultural diversity factors would make impact on the effectiveness of virtual teams by focusing on several success predicators such as leadership (Kayworth & Dorthy, 2000), conflict management (Montoya-Wreiss et al., 2001), communication (Mazneyski & Chudoba, 2000), trust (Jarvenpaa & Leidner, 1999), boundary crossing (Espinosa et al., 2003), norm development, team size (Bradner et al., 2002), creativity (Nemiro, 1998) and technology appropriation (Majchrzak et al., 2000). Additionally, it is vital to get brief understanding about the influence of cultural diversity on the effectiveness of GVT and also to analyse that how Information and Communication Technology (ICT) amplifies or mitigates this influence (Shachal, 2008).

Another aspect which has been seen as challenge for GVT is Communication. It has been directed by many practitioners that this aspect should always need to be managed carefully in accordance to the dimensions of cultural differences (Vinaja, 2004). Correspondingly, it has been analysed that the mode of communication always varies especially in case multi-cultural environment. The significant issue within the virtual teams is that these teams are geographically dispersed and in the frequent cases the members of virtual teams are unaware of the fact how they could address question or to pass on an important information. According to Alexander (2000), virtual team members could adopt two approaches in order to offset this communication. Firstly, they would prefer to phrase their quesntions with attention for the first time and in this way they would keep themselves way from making changes in the sent information. Secondly, they should write clearly and this could be achieved if they don't use acronyms (Alexander, 2000).

Technology is also a big concern for virtual teams. In relation to the state of existing technology, it has been found out that team members located in developed countries are well equipped while most of the members from developing countries does not access to relative new communications and technological infrastructure (Shachal, 2008). However, some other problems (slow computers, incompatible networks, low quality Broadband services and huge network traffic) have been resulted in entitling this aspect as unresolved mystery (Guilherme, 2010).

The language barrier is outlined as obvious problem of virtual teams. This problem occurred because of the reason that all regions (countries) of the world have their own languages (Mazneyski & Chudoba, 2000). And in order to be a member of virtual team, an individual must have to be proficient in speaking other languages as well. It has been identified that the mutual concern of team members upon speaking common languages (English, Spanish, French, Arabic, Chinese and Japanese) could overcome this barrier by far more extent (Vinaja, 2004). But it has been observed that despite of making consensus on common languages, there had been many virtual teams that faced difficulty in overcoming this issue so it meant the role of management is also of great value in resolving this language problem.

It has been observed that companies are increasing adopting the approach of GVT for the purpose of gaining strategic advantage. GVT are categorised as heterogeneous groups of globally dispersed team members that collaborate together with the combination of information technologies and telecommunications for the accomplishment of organisational tasks (Bell & Kozlowski, 2002). However, with the increase of growing implication of such teams it is appearing more significant for the companies in realising that what would makes them successful. Moreover by reviewing past research studies on challenges faced by global virtual teams, it has been discovered that all of studies had been intended on highlighting major issues faced GVT and none of it had tried to investigate issue that how these cultural diversity related challenges are making impact on the effectiveness of communication within GVT (Khosrowpour, 2006). In order to complete this gap, this research study has been conducted.

This research report would examine the influence of cultural diversity and language difference impact on the GVT. It has been discovered from the previous research studies that both aspects are of great significance especially in relation to the effectiveness of knowledge sharing process (Thomas, 2008). And these two aspects could have opposing impact on GVT communication. GVT are characterised by high degree of language diversity & cultural difference and it seemed to be preferable for the purpose of sharing of equivocal knowledge (Khosrowpour, 1998). It has been ascertain that cultural difference and language diversity aspects are directly linked with GVT's knowledge sharing and effectiveness (Schmidt, 2007). However, trust developing factor would results in lessening the intensity of conflicts within GVT

1.2. Aims & Objectives

1.2.1. Aims

The core aim of this research report is to thoroughly examine the aspect of cultural diversity and then to analyse its influence on the effectiveness of communication within Global Virtual Teams (GVT).

1.2.2. Objectives

This research report has four associated objectives, all of those objectives have been outlined below:

- To identify the cultural differences existing among the members of GVT.

- To analyse most frequent cultural challenges that exist in global virtual environment.

- To highlight the contribution of theories on cross-cultural communication so that it would make possible in understanding and recognising the importance of cultural factor within GVT.

- To lean about the role of common speaking languages within GVT.

1.3. Research Questions

- What is basically meant by cultural differences and in what states these differences exist?

- How the theories on cross-cultural communication contribute towards understanding the complications of multi-cultural team work?

- Why some of the challenges (communication problem, weak cohesion and misunderstanding conflicts) occur as a result of cultural difference.

- Does is it possible that the GVT approach of speaking common language useful for them in overcoming the cultural barriers?

1.4. Methodology

This research will be based on secondary data and for this reason the research strategy and therefore case study approach will be adopted. There will be one case study included in this report and in the discussion & analysis section the linkage will be created between the literature review and case study sections. Additionally, on the basis of major findings, some suggestions will be outlined in the recommendation section. A positivism philosophy will be adopted in this research where a testing of an existing theories will be conducted and producing hypothesis for further researches.

Additionally, this research is based on ontology (nature of reality) in its philosophy and it will discuss both reality sides, objectivism and subjectivism. Objectivism as the discussion will generalise the big cultural aspects in the different geographical areas of the world as studied by Hofstedet in his cross cultural communication theory and the overall impact on the function of the global virtual teams. And the subjectivism as the team members individual behaviour to interact with these cultural differences.

However, a deductive approach will be adopted in this research where some areas from existing theories will be examined and specified, moreover some observation will be discussed and confirmed.

1.5. AMP Outcomes

Major outcome of this report is that it would fill research gap by investigating the implications of cultural diversity factors on the communication effectiveness of Global Virtual Teams (GVT). The accomplishment of hard outcomes would be acknowledged if this research report would cover all of the research objectives concerned with this report. Whereas, the attainment of soft outcomes would be known if I would manage to get good grade and for this I will have to work hard.

Chapter-2: Literature Review

In this chapter, the concept of Global Virtual Team will be defined through all the past research studies. Then the significance of cultural difference & cultural diversity factor will be elaborated along with the Hofstede's National Cultural Framework. After describing all these things, certain cultural communication challenges will be defined alongside with the short description of language commonality and its impact on the performance of virtual teams.

2.1. Definition of Virtual Teams

According to Zenun et al. (2007), Virtual Team is a team of people having complementary skills and are working with complete concentrate for the accomplishment of common objectives and hence all of these team members mutually accountable for the end result (Zenun et al., 2007). While, Cascio & Shurygailo (2003) ascertained that virtual teams are form for the purpose of offsetting temporal or geographical separations (Cascio & Shurygailo, 2003). These teams usually woks across the boundaries of space and time with the utilisation of computer driven technologies. Moreover, Anderson et al. (2007) explained that virtual teams are covering broad range of activities and thus it has been determined as advanced form of technology supported working. In general, these teams are composed of individuals who are residing in different parts of the world. It has been inclined that this particular feature meant for the type of computer mediated communicate that make possible for the individuals from different locations to cordinate and integrate their individual inouts and efforts (Peters & Manz, 2007).

According to Gassmann et al. (2003), a virtual team is a collaboration of individuals where each group member interacts through interdependent tasks directed by the common objective and this team works across links that are strengthened through several aspects (communication, information and multimedia technologies). Hertel et al. (2005) called virtual teams as distributed work teams as all of its members are geographically dispersed and coordinate more significally through comminication technologies and electronic information (Hertel et al., 2005). Therefore, Lurey & Rasinghani (2001) emphasised on the point that virtual teams are the groups of employees who are working together despite of the fact they are dispersed across organisational boundaries. Powell et al. (2004) defined virtual teams as group of organisationally, time and geographical dispersed individuals come together through information technologies for the execution and accomplishment of one or more organisational tasks and goals.

2.2. Why Global Virtual Teams?

It has been learned that the motive behind Global Virtual Teams (GVT) is very much similar to the excitement behind team work trend realised during the period of 1980s. It has been found the companies don't put these teams simply in command and expect ordinary performance from them. There must be the motive of capitalising the benefits of this approach (Zayani, 2008) However, the development and management of GVT needs investment of about similar level and if it would be done correctly then it could deliver more benefits and value to the given company than the traditional teams (Pinjani, 2007).

2.2.1. Advantages of Going Global

- It has been inclined that the GVT results in fancy the chance of entering the global markets and thus outcome in form of giving access to hire best talent of those markets (Garton & Wegryn, 2006).

- If the company would manage to successfully break through conflicts caused by the diversity factor then it enable the company to get advantage of new thoughts and perspectives that would direct the given company towards enhanced innovation (Duarte & Snyder, 2011).

- As a fact of global makeup of GVT, local team members would have possibility to emerge as experts and representatives in the global markets (Khosrowpour, 2001).

2.2.2. Advantages of Going Virtual

- It has been determined that through the leveraging of GVT, the company would intend themselves in keeping travel expenses at minimum level alongside enjoying the benefits of employing team members from different countries and also having different perspectives (Hellriegel & Slocum, 2010).

- Communication through email or other multimedia technologies permits team members to respond rapidly and thus lead them towards more thoughtful responses (Settle-Murphy, 2013).

- Technology solutions based on global linked perspective would result in giving direct access to team members to required information. It meant that all associated documents will be available at short hand and also would team members to deal with all kind of challenges 24/7 (Puffer, 2004).

However, leveraging all above advantages would not only offer virtual edge to the company but also could help them in outperforming its competitors.

2.3. What is meant by Cultural Difference?

There have been large number of research studies undergone for the purpose of understanding cultural differences (Weisinger & Salipante, 2000; Brannen & Salk, 2000). However, it has been believed that this concept in helpful for the better understanding of certain challenges that could be occurred in multicultural settings (Brett & Kern, 2006). The concept of cultural difference is constructed for explaining certain dissimilarities exist in relation to culture's aspects: ethics, norms, beliefs, core values, rituals & customs, and legal, economic & political systems (Adler, 2008). In general, the term cultural difference is used for the representation of challenges to knowledge sharing, communication effectiveness and exchange of complicated idea notions (Stahl et al., 2010). It has been learned from previous case studies on GVT that cultural difference could have positive impact on knowledge sharing as the component of intercultural encounter intends to make tacit and contextual knowledge as explicit (Earley & Mosakowski, 2000). In this regard, it is of significance to differentiate between the sharing of canonical and equivocal knowledge respectively. The blend of advanced media and ambivalent & complex knowledge that need to be shared is more expect5 to be beneficial. This situation would even be more vital where the cultural differences between involved team members are outspoken and as a reason of this extensive and broad communication they would understand each other cultural values. Moreover, it appears believable that once rich media set-up linked with canonical knowledge then it could provide a pointless excess of culture cues hindering understanding (Klitmøller & Lauring, 2013). Therefore, one may assume that lean media would be more effective and efficient for the sharing of canonical knowledge within the teams comprised of individuals who have great cultural difference among themselves.

2.4. What is meant by Intercultural Competence?

Intercultural competence is the capability composed of knowledge & skills that helps individual in interacting successfully with people belongs to other national, religious, cultural and geographical groups (Deardorff, 2009). Specifically, when someone has high degree of intercultural competence then it meant that he/she has better idea about how to interact with people from other social groups. This aspect emphasised on the fact that a person must need to be curious (sensitive) about the cultural differences and should also need to alter his/her behaviour as a sign of respect for other cultures (Hammer et al., 2003).

2.5. Global Virtual Teams & Intercultural Competence

Intercultural competence is considered as comparatively unexamined factor of GVT. It has been observed that most of the research undergone on virtual teaming is emphasised more either on identifying similar characteristics of GVT to face to face teams or on examining that how technological (virtual) environment would have an impact on the effectiveness of GVT (Byram et al., 2001). In order to resolve this issue, it has been ascertained that the focus on intercultural may results in enhancing the effectiveness of GVT. It has been predicted that if the team members of GVT have high degree of intercultural competence then following situations will occur (Amant & Kelsey, 2012):

- Overall team's capability of performing tasks will be improved (enhanced task performance).

- The team's ability of exchanging and understanding communication will be enhanced (enhanced overall communication).

- The team's overall engagement will be increased (Katzenbach & Smith, 1999).

Moreover, it has been determined that there is a direct relationship exist between ability of team members interacting with others and the degree of team performance and effectiveness (Moodian, 2008). However, it has been observed that despite of this fact organisations are not seriously focusing on signify intercultural competence as a vital aspect. Organisations are unable to cultivate their virtual team members' intercultural competence and correspondingly neglect this factor (high degree of intercultural competence) especially during the time of recruitment. Hence, it has been discovered that the influence of intercultural competence is great on the effectiveness of GVT. If there is a case that team members don't understand that how to admire the importance of cultural diversity then they would not able to create reasonable roadmap. It could also be resulted in misperceptions and results in delaying project finishing time (Byram, 2003).

2.6. Global Virtual Teams & Cultural Diversity

From the previous research studies, it has been shown that the cultural diversity factor would play significant role in forming and shaping group processes and interaction patterns within GVT (Jarvenpaa & Leidner, 1998). Moreover, Jarvenpaa & Leidner (1998) contended that the factor of cultural diversity is useful in developing trust between all involveeam members. But some researchers had opposed this pointed and have pointed out that too much reliance of GVT on email and other related means of communications mitigate the influence of cultural diversity. Additionally, they have contended that the cultural diversity factor is no longer remains a noticeable aspect. But some research reports claimed that the increasing need for diverse modes of communication have been resulted in making an impact on cultural diversity (Sembdner., 2011). It has been cleared through the research finding of one report which outlined that virtual team members involved in engineering design and prototyping asked for the requirement of visiting each other places on extensive basis so that it would assimilate the organisational and cultural context (Cutkosky et al., 1996). And this initiative as an outcome permitted more effective communication (MacGregor, 2007).

In regard to research findings on cross-cultural virtual teams, it has been determined that virtual teams' focus on various contexts that differences in term of socialisation processes outcome in different cultures (Terpstra & David, 1991). Therefore, differences in national culture, organisational settings and professional training could have an influence on certain aspects: Project Progress, Media Choices and Group

Processes (De Meyer, 1991). A global virtual team is by definition is culturally disparate. It has been understood that people only acquire shared understanding when they are correspondingly socialised in cultural priorities for action, cultural classifications and cultural codes for conduct (Terpstra & David, 1991). While, there are some sub-teams that have dispersed teams and these are socialised on the basis of different national and organisational cultures despite of the fact that they share considerably similar professional culture. Cultural Disparity meant that all team members engaged in virtual teams not only have to share work practices but also must have to create norms (based on mutual understanding) for the purpose of interaction. Cultural diversity is not essentially a cause of project failure and in majority cases it had been determined as major source of competitive edge (Lipnack & Stamps, 2000). It is important to mention that when the virtual team is composed of members belong to dispersed location for the objective of coordinating their activity then they could produce synergy from this cultural diversity factor and hence enhance project performance (Heneman & Greenberger, 2002). On the other side, cultural miscommunication could disrupt coordination aspect and then would have negative impact on project performance.

2.7. Cross-Cultural Communication Theories

In regard to cross-cultural communication theories, the model proposed by Hofstede (1996) always ranked at the top. He came up with five funtamental dimensions that are briefly discussed below:

2.7.1. Hierarchy

This dimension is also known as power distance. It is directly related to the aspect that to how much extent people belong to each culture accept s the unequal distribution of power (Neelankavil, 2004). There are cultures that prefer hierarchy and concentrate more on leader status (people in these cultures need direction from the leader and also think that leader will only have an authority to make decision as well). Moreover, it has been predicted that individuals of these cultures would accept the rules imposed by the leaders and on the other hand the questioning authority would only be discouraged (Taras et al., 2010).

While, there are cultures on the other side that are intended more on the team involvement and broad consultation. The group decision making is more frequent within these cultures. Questioning authority within these cultures are more likely to be accepted and encouraged (Wei-hsin, 2005).

2.7.2. Ambiguity

This dimension is also termed as Uncertainty Avoidance and it is more focused on examininf the fact that how an individual feels comfortable during ambigious situation (Piepenburg, 2011). In relation to this dimension, there are some cultures that encourages the risk taking nature and people always stay confortable in regard to approaching new or different approaches. On the other hand, there are cultures that emphasise more on three aspects (routine, formality and regulation). Additionally, it has been determined that people belong to these cultures would only go for tested or tried way of doing things instead of experimenting with unfamiliar methodologies (Hofstede et al., 1990).

2.7.3. Individualism

This dimension is more intended on the measuring the fact that to how much extent an indvidual is self determined (Luger, 2009). In relation to individualistic cultures, people are only concerned about individual success and most of the time an individual take care of oneself. On the other hand, there are cultures that place more values on two things: group loyalty and group interest (Barkema & Vermeulen, 1997).

2.7.4. Achievement Orientation

This dimension is also named as Masculinity vs. Femininity. This dimension is directly linked with the gender aspect of specified cultures (Hofstede, 2002). It has been inclined that the cultures where the masculinity factor dominates, then it meant that these cultures are appeared to be achievement oriented hence these cultures assign value to certain factors (achievement, success and money). While according to Hofstede & Minkov (2010), the cultures that assign vale to femininity aspect are assumed to assign value towards certain things (interpersonal harmony, quality of life and sharing of thoughts).

2.7.5. Long term Orientation

This dimension is intended on measuring the extent of orientation of cultures in relation to long term rewards and short term gains (Hofstede, 2001). It has been found that at one end continuum, there are cultures that intend more on long term rewards. And on the other end, there are cultures that only focused towards short term gains (Hofstede, 2011).

According to Hofstede (1980), cultural values are reflected across all of the five dimensions within a continuum. It has been assumed that individuals' behaviours and expectations are more probably be prejudiced by their respective country's cultural values and traits (Schimmack et al., 2005). According to this framework, team members who ranked low on power distance index, uncertainty avoidance while categorised high in term of individualism are expected to have certain characteristics:

- More likely to participate actively in deciding over the direction of teams.
- Always ready question team leader's decisions.
- Comfortable with pursuing different approaches.
- Intended on accomplishing their own goals with the perspective that it would giving useful support in facilitating group's success (Magnusson et al., 2008).

While on the other side, individuals belongs to other cultures who high on power distance index and low on the individualism dimension are expected to have following characteristics:

- Formal and hierarchical team structure and put more emphasis on leadership aspect.
- Always tried to be disciplined and structured.
- Intended more on assisting other members within a team so that it would enable that specified team in accomplishing its projected objectives (Rottig et al., 2013).

Therefore ir has been inclined that Hofstede's cultural framework is helpful in thinking that how misunderstanding would occur within Global Virtual Teams (GVT). This point will also be understood through the scenario that if someone belongs to the culture which values hierarchy becomes leader of given virtual team and it would be predicted that he would make decision without creating consent among all team members. And in the way, it would make negative impact on the relationship existing between the team leader and team members as they were expecting to be consulted before the time of making decision.

2.8. Cultural Challenges faced by Global Virtual Teams (GVT)

Despite of large number of benefits, it has been observed that GVT are subject to certain cultural challenges. All of these challenges are described below:

2.8.1. Communication Challenge

Communication is always consider as significant aspect in human activities. In relation to GVT, communication challenges frequently make impact on the effectiveness of virtual teams in the form of reducing the sharing of information and arising of interpersonal conflicts (Pauleen, 2004). It is evident that GVT adopts clear or direct communication approach especially for the purpose of organising group meeting. And this approach is considered as western approach. But on the other hand, it has been determined that team members from high context cultures most of the time prefer to go for indirect communication mode. They do thing by asking questions instead of making direct point during project or collaboration meetings. Moreover, if there would be a case that the team members failed to understand such communication then the differing team members could preceive it as a voilation of their cultural ethics & norms and it would smear the relationship and collaboration exists among the team members (Nemiro et al., 2008).

2.8.2. Accent & Fluency Challenge

English language is extensively categorised as international business & collaboration language. Despite of this fact, frustation and misunderstanding would occur in GVT, And the main reason would be the non native english speakers. And as an outcome of this problem, native english speakers would find in understanding them because non fluency and accent of english language. It has been observed that non-native speakers have many thoughts in their mind to share but they unable to express it because of their incompetence in speaking english fluently (Gibson & Cohen, 2003). This is considers as prominent challenge being faced by GVT while communicating with team members from other cultures. This problem could inhibits virtual teams in expressing their competency and expertise with others and then it would results in creating frustation amongst the teams.

2.8.3. Attitude Challenge

In relation to the hierarchical context, team members from low context cultures seem to be flexible or obtainable in their approach however this thing is not true for team members belong to high context cultures. It has been expected that organisations would treat these individuals (from high context cultures) in accordance with their assigned role or status within a team. And this practice would intend other team members to feel uncomfortable. Hence, as an impact failure of some team members (who are not intended with this approach) in giving to such expectations could be resulted in causing humiliation amongst team. Therefore, it has been seen that admiting hierarchy approah is strictly being followed within Asian cultures.

2.8.4. Decision Making Challenge

Because of cultural difference, the conflict in decision making process would also be classified as major challenge which used to be faced by GVT during collaboration. The factor of decision making depends hugely upon the extent that how rapidly decisions are made and how much analysis is needed (Zofi, 2011). This problem could be illustrated with a example that if there is someone who intends to make decision quickly would get frustrated while working with those who are used to of spending much time in making decisions. Similarly it could be understood as a fact that there some people who are oriented towards thinking before making any sort of decision but this phenomenon is not same with other people from different cultures. While, the tolerance factor would play a significant role in avoding that confrontation (Jones et al., 2005).

2.8.5. Lack of Awareness

It has been understood that GVT are extensively categorised under the tag of awareness deficits. A large number of researches have discovered various problems that originated from the fact specifically during the situation when team member are collocated and also are unaware of each other traits and potential (Nataatmadja & Dyson, 2006). And there is a much chance that it would make negative on GVT's project work (Lewkowicz et al., 2008). Additionally because of this issue, there would be special effort required tp update each remote team members about the progress of work which hence results in influencing the effectiveness of team work (Mäkilouko, 2004).

2.8.6. Inability in Building Social Bonds

It has been believed that dependence alone on mediated amd asynchronous interactions inhibit the creation of solid working relationships among team members. There is a speculation that GVT approach of under-emphasising on social and members' well being factors is the main cause of keeping team members far from performing well (Stewart, 1994). Theories on media richness and social presence have pointed out that mediated comunication system's inherent limitations constrain social interactions (Distefano & Maznevski, 2000). Many research stufies on virtual teams have made it clear that team members engaged in GVT most of the time had difficulty in building strong working relationships (Mowshowitz, 1997). Therefore, it has been inclined that geographic separation hindered team members' abilities in developing relationships with managers, co-workers and customers (Johnson, 1999).

2.8.7. Lack of Trust

It has been determined that the challenge faced by virtual teams in forming social relationships may forced them towards another challenge known lack of trust. According to Jarvenpaa et al. (1998), development of trust is always seems as major factor for virtual team's success. While too much reliance of GVT on mediated communication intended them towards the issue of lack of trust (Jarvenpaa & Leidner, 1998).

2.8.8. Lack of Agreement

It has been inclined that GVT would find it difficult in reaching agreement on certain movements or situations that need immediate action. The worse situation may occur when GVT tend to freign agreement with an intension of avoiding any further needs for collaboration and would find it useful to go with potentially inferior solution (Lipnack & Stamps, 2000). In relation to the organisational settings, it has been proved that this problem of lack of agreement would not only reduce the given virtual team's motivation and commitment level but also would lessen the chances of successful take-up make by external customers.

In short, it has been predicted that all above cultural challenges being faced by GVT would impede virtual teams' capabilities in accomplishing their tasks and projects.

2.9. Language Commonality

Language had been determined as forgotten factor specifically from the perspective of International Business Research studies (Steyaert et al., 2011). While, because of increasing globalisation the significance for this theme has been growing (Piekkari & Tietze, 2011). And now in relation to Multinational Corporations' (MNCs) merits study, it widely acknowledged as stand-alone topic instead of being a part of cultural difference (Barner-Rasmussen & Aarnio, 2011). It has been revealed that sharing of common language results in increasing knowledge sharing and communication frequency within MNCs (Welch & Welch, 2008). In regard to GVT, language commonality states to the degree to which individuals have common understanding of English language involving certain skills[1] and knowledge about its applicability (Cle´ment & Gardner, 2001). Moreover, shared language commonality not only denotes members' linguistic proficiency significantly of English language but also refers to the extent to which virtual team members own overlapping styles and knowledge about communication (frequently used phrases, vocabulary, accents and spellings). The fact is that English is frequently the common language of Multinational Corporations' (MNCs) employees engaged in GVT but still there are variations in term of style and proficiency level exist among team members.

---

[1] Proficiency in speaking & listening, conventions and grammatical structure.

Chapter-3: Case Study, Analysis & Discussion

In this chapter, Virtual teaming practices of BakBone Software Inc. will be discussed in combination with the cross-cultural communication and cultural difference challenges that are being faced by the company. Additionally, this case study also incorporates the company's approach of getting rid of these challenges. Then on the basis case study, the link will try to be created between all previous chapters in the discussion section.

3.1. Case Study on BakBone Software
3.1.1. Company Profile
BakBone Software is a global company for supplying software solution for professional data protection. The company is also renowned for offering sales & marketing support of IT (Information Technology) products in Nordic market. The company has centralised setup along with decentralised employee base. Company's virtual team is functioning despite of the fact that it has been separated by various aspects (multiple time zones, distance and national cultures).

3.1.2. Motivation behind the Adoption of Virtual Team
Normally there are two major reasons (recruitment & necessity) behind the approach of virtual teams. In relation to software solution industry, it has been determined that all firms are following the trend of creating dispersed technical support centers. And the core objective behind the formulation of virtual teams is to function consistently around the clock. However, it has also been found out that the recruitment over broader geographic area meant for the overcoming of labour shortage issue.

According to the management of BakBone Software, the main reason behind the company's decision to go after virtual team is that the company found it hard in recruiting competent professions specifically those who want to start work from 2; 00 AM significantly during Saturday & Sunday. The company opting for virtual teaming with the purpose of having massive and professional staff at one place. Currently BakBone has employed 13 professionals in its technical support cent and it has been observed that all team members have computer science degrees. And in this way, the company is enjoying the benefits of employing talented people from different countries and it also results in providing superior services to its customers on a consistent basis.

3.1.3. Cross-Cultural Communication

According to company's strategic level management, the experience of virtual team is going well because the company is giving special attention towards the controlling and managing of communication & information sharing elements. And for communication purposes, company is very conscious in regard to take account of cultural difference factor.

But despite of such things, the company is facing some communication problems. For example, BakBone Software's management found out that their Japanese members despite of the fact that they could communicate fluently in English but still hesitate in speaking with other members. And the management perceived that they are not communicating with other cultures group members because they think they are not much good in speaking and listening English. As an outcome of this kind of behaviour, Japanese members stay quiet during conference calls. This situation has directed BakBone Software's towards organising conference calls with their Japanese fellows separately. And in order to off-set this problem, BakBone Software management is focusing more on the development of savvy communications skills so that it would intend the company to carry on its practices of working across cultural boundaries.

3.1.3.   Cultural Difference

In addition to cross-cultural challenge, the company has also undergone through Cultural Difference problem. The company's team members from the company's virtual team of software development are from US and Israel. However, it has been found that its Israeli team members are not willing to work on Friday due to religious purpose and thus putting results leaving US team members in isolation. In order to overcome this problem, BakBone software Inc. has made this compulsory for the new hiring that they would have to call-on also on Friday so that the company's sales force and customers remain in touch.

3.1.4. Performance Evaluation

It has been seen that management of BakBone Software Inc. is not much worried about the evaluation process of their employees' performance. In this regard, company has implement certain Information Systems which record the time each employee at support center takes in resolving the problems of customers.

3.1.5. Findings

It has been observed that despite of certain cross-cultural communication and cultural differences issues, BakBone Software Inc. has managed to perform at satisfactory level. And the company attribute such success to the fact that all of team members have interaction with each other on continuous basis. And this has intended them to remain informed about each other strengths and thus results in developing and maintaining great extent of trust.

3.2. Analysis

This research report has thoroughly examined the influence of cultural diversity and language difference impact on the GVT. From the literature review chapter, it has been understood that both aspects are of great significance especially in relation to the effectiveness of knowledge sharing process. And these two aspects could have opposing impact on GVT communication. GVT are characterised by high degree of language diversity & cultural difference and it seemed to be preferable for the purpose of sharing of equivocal knowledge. And communication is predicted to be as much effective as it used to be in traditional teams. However, there are two problems (lack of sufficient information and misinterpretation) that could be resulted in arising conflicts within GVT. In some cases, it has been found out when team members looked to resolve cultural challenges would encounter certain language challenges. The main reason of this issue could be absence of language commonality factor. It has been assumed that lean media permit team members in reflecting upon their writing mistakes and would be instrumental for the removal of certain verbal cues that could increase the possibility of misunderstandings. In short, lean media increases equivocal knowledge which then decreases miscommunications and uncertainty elements.

It has been proved that cultural difference and language diversity aspects are directly linked with GVT's knowledge sharing and effectiveness. However, trust developing factor would not only resulted in lessening the intensity of conflicts within GVT but also would enhance their effectiveness. In relation to the shared language concept, it has been discovered that if there would be a case that the extent of using of common language is too much then it is ascertain that the leanness in the selected communication media would intend GVT to be more effective. But research reports outlined that language commonality would have moderate impact on the knowledge sharing process. And this argument is supported through the difference existed in term of language accent and proficiency. Additionally, the use of advanced technology has added more challenges to the culturally distinct communication behaviour. It is important to mention that face to face communication (through video conference) within GVT would be more effective for the sharing of equivocal knowledge and on the other hand language diversity factor would have negative influence on organizational communication. Finally, it is significant to highlight that intercultural communication indicates the existence of conflicting relationship between culture difference and common language use.

It has been analysed from the above case study that BakBone Software Inc. has been facing two serious problems. First problem is linked with the approach of cross-cultural communication, where it has been identified by the company's management that their Japanese team members are hesitating in term of expressing their opinions and suggestions. And the situation like this happened because they believe that they would unable to express their opinion in the right context of English speaking mode. However, the second problem is related to the perspective of cultural difference where the company's team members located in Israel are unwilling to work on Friday which creates trouble for the company in communicating with them on that particular day and made negative impact on the quality of services being provided to their customers. For the purpose of resolving first problem, the company has adopted the approach of holding video conference with their Japanese members separately. And for the purpose of resolving second problem, the company has made new hiring and also made essential for them to stay available for communication also on Friday. In this way, company's management have intended them in stay in touch with themselves and also with customers all the time.

3.3. Discussion

From previous chapters, it has been discovered that the factor of cultural diversity would create issues for two major dimensions (Trust and Effective Communication) of team effectiveness. Moreover, an understanding of cultural diversity impact is not only significant for team effectiveness bur also for knowledge creation aspect as well. It has been believed that establishing & maintaining trust within GVT would prove to be defining initiative for the team effectiveness. One could understand this point in a way that in order to collaborate effectively & efficiently, team members should trust each other and this could be done through the monitoring of each other activities. Additionally, trust would also be established and maintained through team members' ethical behaviour and this would only be possible with the formulation of codes of conduct. Therefore, it has been determined that the element of team consistency would play an important part in maintaining level of trust among team members. But for attainting this thing, same team members would have to participate collectively for longer duration. So, it meant that accomplishing team consistency is not an easy task.

It has been learned that the corporations that have virtual teams would be in strong position in enjoying the advantages of having global access. The reason behind this aspect that if a corporation employed individuals from different nations then if means that each individual would have better idea of his/her country's economy & business situation and in this manner a corporation would utilise the opportunity of either procuring raw of low cost or employing human resource of same competency at relatively lower salaries It has been ascertained that GVT bring different cultures on single platform with the intension of gaining competitive advantage of entering other countries' markets or supplying its marketing offerings (products or services) on global context. Significantly, GVT is instrumental in the cases where there would be risk in enforcing people with same cultural backgrounds to work together.

It has been discovered that various multicultural problems could be occurred due to cultural differences and language aspects. Increasing trend of virtual working and the development of advance communication tools meant that more and more people would face the problem of working across cultures. It has been seen that GVT intend people to contact with individual belong to different cultural and environmental context. So, it has been suggested that corporations that encourage virtual team working must demonstrate the way of dealing with cultural factor which could have direct influence on various components (team performance, dynamics and trust). It has been found out that there are still many factors that are embedded within GVT need to be improvised so that it would enable GVT to become successful.

Moreover in relation to research objective-1, it has been identified from the previous research studies on the approach of GVT that cultural difference could have positive impact on knowledge sharing as the component of intercultural encounter intends to make tacit and contextual knowledge as explicit. Therefore, one may assume that lean media would be more effective and efficient for the sharing of canonical knowledge within the teams comprised of individuals who have great cultural difference among themselves. While in regard to research objective-2, it has been analysed that there are various challenges GVT (Communication Challenge, Accent & Fluency Challenge, Attitude Challenge, Decision Making Challenge, Lack of Awareness, Inability in Building Social Bonds, Lack of Trust and Lack of Agreement) that could be faced by GVT. In short, it has been predicted that all of these cultural challenges being faced by GVT would impede virtual teams' capabilities in accomplishing their tasks and projects.

With respect to research objective-3, the framework formulated by Hofstede (1980) is very useful in directing individuals that how should one could distinguish among the characteristics of each other cultures. And in this way it would help GVT in respecting each other norms and values that would have positive impact on the teams' project management approach in shape of enhancing teams' effectiveness and efficiency level. Finally in regard to research objective-4, it has been learned that the sharing of common language results in increasing knowledge sharing and communication frequency within MNCs. While in regard to GVT, language commonality states to the degree to which individuals have common understanding of English language involving certain skills and knowledge about its applicability. Moreover, shared language commonality not only denotes members' linguistic proficiency significantly of English language but also refers to the extent to which virtual team members own overlapping styles and knowledge about communication (frequently used phrases, vocabulary, accents and spellings).

Chapter-4: Conclusion & Recommendations

In this chapter, major points of this report will be outlined. Correspondingly, this report will also contain certain recommendations that the management of the company should follow in order to stay away from all the potential consequences. The topic for the future research study will also be suggested in this section so that it would add value to the existing research material on the concept of Global Virtual Teams. .

4.1. Conclusion

It has been concluded that Global Virtual Team is determined as a collaboration of individuals where each group member interacts through interdependent tasks directed by the common objective and this team works across links that are strengthened through several aspects (communication, information and multimedia technologies). On the other hand, it has been believed that the concept of cultural difference is helpful for the better understanding of certain challenges that could be occurred in multicultural settings. Moreover, this concept of cultural difference is constructed for explaining certain dissimilarities exist in relation to culture's aspects: ethics, norms, beliefs, core values, rituals & customs, and legal, economic & political systems. In general, the term cultural difference is used for the representation of challenges to knowledge sharing, communication effectiveness and exchange of complicated idea notions. It has been learned from previous case studies on GVT that cultural difference could have positive impact on knowledge sharing as the component of intercultural encounter intends to make tacit and contextual knowledge as explicit.

From the previous research studies, it has been shown that the cultural diversity factor would play significant role in forming and shaping group processes and interaction patterns within GVT. Moreover, it has been contended that the factor of cultural diversity is useful in developing trust between all involved members. But some researchers had opposed this pointed and have pointed out that too much reliance of GVT on email and other related means of communications mitigate the influence of cultural diversity. Additionally, they have contended that the cultural diversity factor is no longer remains a noticeable aspect. But some research reports claimed that the increasing need for diverse modes of communication have been resulted in making an impact on cultural diversity.

In regard to cross-cultural communication theories, the model proposed by Hofstede (1996) always ranked at the top. The dimension known as power distance. is directly related to the aspect that to how much extent people belong to each culture accept s the unequal distribution of power. The dimension termed as Uncertainty Avoidance is more focused on examininf the fact that how an individual feels comfortable during ambigious situation. The dimension called as Indicidualism is more intended on the measuring the fact that to how much extent an indvidual is self determined. The dimension named as Masculinity vs. Femininity is directly linked with the gender aspect of specified cultures. This dimension known as Long Term Orientation is intended on measuring the extent of orientation of cultures in relation to long term rewards and short term gains.

Despite of large number of benefits, it has been observed that GVT are subject to certain cultural challenges. In relation to GVT, communication challenges frequently make impact on the effectiveness of virtual teams in the form of reducing the sharing of information and arising of interpersonal conflicts. Accent & Fluency challenge considers as prominent challenge being faced by GVT while communicating with team members from other cultures. This problem could inhibits virtual teams in expressing their competency and expertise with others and then it would results in creating frustation amongst the teams. Because of cultural difference, the conflict in decision making process would also be classified as major challenge which used to be faced by GVT during collaboration. It has been understood that GVT are extensively categorised under the tag of awareness deficits. A large number of researches have discovered various problems that originated from the fact specifically during the situation when team member are collocated and also are unaware of each other traits and potential Many research stufies on virtual teams have made it clear that team members engaged in GVT most of the time had difficulty in building strong working relationships. Therefore, it has been determined that the challenge faced by virtual teams in forming social relationships may forced them towards another challenge known lack of trust It has been inclined that GVT would also find it difficult in reaching agreement on certain movements or situations that need immediate action.

It has been analysed from the case study of BakBone Software Inc. that the company has been facing two serious problems. First problem is linked with the approach of cross-cultural communication, where it has been identified by the company's management that their Japanese team members are hesitating in term of expressing their opinions and suggestions. And the second problem is related to the perspective of cultural difference where the company's team members located in Israel are unwilling to work on Friday which creates trouble for the company in communicating with them on that particular day and made negative impact on the quality of services being provided to their customers. It has been observed that despite of certain cross-cultural communication and cultural differences issues, BakBone Software Inc. has managed to perform at satisfactory level. And the company attribute such success to the fact that all of team members have interaction with each other on continuous basis. And this has intended them to remain informed about each other strengths and thus results in developing and maintaining great extent of trust. It has been revealed that sharing of common language results in increasing knowledge sharing and communication frequency within MNCs. In regard to GVT, language commonality states to the degree to which individuals have common understanding of English language involving certain skills[2] and knowledge about its applicability.

Moreover in relation to research objective-1, it has been identified from the previous research studies on the approach of GVT that cultural difference could have positive impact on knowledge sharing as the component of intercultural encounter intends to make tacit and contextual knowledge as explicit. While in regard to research objective-2, it has been analysed that there are various challenges GVT (Communication Challenge, Accent & Fluency Challenge, Attitude Challenge, Decision Making Challenge, Lack of Awareness, Inability in Building Social Bonds, Lack of Trust and Lack of Agreement) that could be faced by GVT). With respect to research objective-3, the framework formulated by Hofstede (1980) is very useful in

---

[2] Proficiency in speaking & listening, conventions and grammatical structure.

directing individuals that how should one could distinguish among the characteristics of each other cultures. And in this way it would help GVT in respecting each other norms and values that would have positive impact on the teams' project management approach in shape of enhancing teams' effectiveness and efficiency level. Finally in regard to research objective-4, it has been learned that the sharing of common language results in increasing knowledge sharing and communication frequency within MNCs.

This research report has thoroughly examined the influence of cultural diversity and language difference impact on the GVT. It has been understood that both aspects are of great significance especially in relation to the effectiveness of knowledge sharing process. And these two aspects could have opposing impact on GVT communication. GVT are characterised by high degree of language diversity & cultural difference and it seemed to be preferable for the purpose of sharing of equivocal knowledge. It has been proved that cultural difference and language diversity aspects are directly linked with GVT's knowledge sharing and effectiveness. However, trust developing factor would results in lessening the intensity of conflicts within GVT

4.2. Recommendations

This research report would seems to have useful contribution in relation to aspect of Cultural Diversity issue and its Implications on the Communication over Global Virtual Team (GVT). It has been recommended that the company's managers need to be aware all cultural issues that could cause problem to the communication aspect within Global Virtual Teams. Relatedly, virtual corporations should have to understand the importance diversity factor in relation to adopt the approach of GVT. And if the specified corporation would manage to develop trust among team members then the communication element will become sampler. Correspondingly, company's managers also need to ensure that all members within GVT are contributing on equal terms and are gaining the benefit from having interaction in the form of team meetings. In some cases, managers need to guide and direct their virtual team members as well. It has been discovered that virtual teams would face more challenges than traditional teams (those who have physical interaction). However, these challenges could be off-set through effective communication.

Managers could establish certain policies and procedures in order to form and maintain satisfactory form of working environment.

For future perspective, one could conduct research on investigating the key success factors of multi-cultural virtual teams. It has been predicted that the research report on the suggested topic will be resulted in enhancing the available knowledge of GVT. From the implication perspective, it would have two implications: understanding various managerial issues in GVT and benefiting Information System (IS) researchers & practitioners.

Chapter-5: References

Adler, N.J., 2008. *International dimensions of organisational behaviour*. 5th ed. Mason: South Western Publishing.

Alexander, S., 2000. Virtual Teams Going Global. *InfoWorld*, 22(46), pp.55-56.

Amant, K.S. & Kelsey, , 2012. *Computer-mediated Communication Across Cultures: International Interactions in Online Environments*. New York: Information Science Reference.

Anderson , A.H., Mcewan, R., Bal, J. & Carletta, J., 2007. Virtual team meetings: An analysis of communication and context. *Computers in Human Behaviour*, 23(1), pp.2558-2580.

Barkema, H.G. & Vermeulen, F., 1997. What differences in the cultural backgrounds of partners are detrimental for international joint ventures?. *Journal of International Business Studies*, 28(1), pp.845–64.

Barner-Rasmussen, W. & Aarnio, C., 2011. Shifting the faultlines of language: A quantitative functional-level exploration of language use in MNC subsidiaries. *Journal of World Business, 46: 288–295*, 46(1), pp.288–95.

Bell, B.S. & Kozlowski, S.W.J., 2002. A Typology of Virtual Teams: Implications for Effective Leadership. *Group & Organization Management*, 27(1), pp.14–49.

Bradner, E., Mark, G. & Hertel, T.D., 2002. *Effects of team size on participation, awareness, and technology choice in geographically distributed teams, in Proceedings of the 35th Hawaii International Conference on Systems Sciences*. Hawaii.

Brannen, M.Y. & Salk, J.E., 2000. Partnering across borders: Negotiating organizational culture in a German–Japanese joint venture. *Human Relations*, 53(1), pp.451–88.

Brett, J..B. & Kern, , 2006. Managing multicultural teams. *Harvard Business Review*, 84(1), pp.84–92.

Byram, M., 2003. *Intercultural Competence*. Council of Europe.

Byram, , Nichols, & Stevens, , 2001. *Developing Intercultural Competence in Practice*. New York: Multilingual Matters.

Cascio, W.F. & Shurygailo, S., 2003. E-Leadership and Virtual Teams. *Organisational Dynamics*, 31(1), pp.362-76.

Cle´ment, R. & Gardner, R.C., 2001. Second language mastery. In W.P. Robinson & P. Giles , eds. *The new handbook of language and social psychology*. New York: John Wiley & Sons Ltd. pp.489–504.

Cutkosky, M.R., Tenenbaum, J.M. & Glicksman, J.M., 1996. CCollaborative engineering over the Internet. *Communications of the ACM*, 39(9), pp.78-87.

De Meyer, A., 1991. Tech talk: How managers are simulating global R&D communication. *Sloan Management Review*, 32(3), pp.49-58.

Deardorff, D.K., 2009. *The SAGE Handbook of Intercultural Competence*. London: SAGE.

Distefano, J.J. & Maznevski, M.I., 2000. Creating value with diverse teams in global management. *Organizational Dynamics*, 29(1), pp.45-63.

Duarte, D.L. & Snyder, N.T., 2011. *Mastering Virtual Teams: Strategies, Tools, and Techniques That Succeed*. San Francisco: John Wiley & Sons.

Earley, P.C. & Mosakowski, E., 2000. Creating hybrid team cultures: An empirical test of transnational team functioning. *Academy of Management Journal*, 43(1), pp.26–49.

Espinosa, J.A., Cumming, J.N., Wilson, J.M. & Pearce, B.M., 2003. Team boundary issues across multiple global firms. *Journal of Management Information Systems*, 19(4), pp.157-90.

Garton, & Wegryn, , 2006. *Managing Without Walls: Maximize Success with Virtual, Global, and Cross-Cultural Teams*. MC Press.

Gassmann, O., Zedtwit & Zedtwitz, M.V., 2003. Trends and determinants of managing virtual R&D teams. *Brand Management*, 33(1), pp.243-62.

Gibson, C.B. & Cohen, S.G., 2003. *Virtual Teams That Work: Creating Conditions for Virtual Team Effectiveness*. San Francisco: John Wiley & Sons.

Goldman, J.E., 2000. *Applied Data Communications*. New York: John Wiley and Sons, Inc.

Guilherme, M., 2010. *The Intercultural Dynamics of Multicultural Working*. Multilingual Matters.

Hammer, M.R., Bennett, M.J. & Wiseman, R., 2003. Measuring Intercultural Sensitivity: The Intercultural Development Inventory. *International Journal of Intercultural Relations*, 27(4), pp.421-43.

Hellriegel, & Slocum, , 2010. *Organizational Behavior*. 13th ed. Mason: Cengage Learning.

Heneman, R.L. & Greenberger, D.B., 2002. *Human Resource Management in Virtual Organizations*. New York: IAP.

Hertel, G.T., Geister, S. & Konradt, U., 2005. Managing virtual teams: A review of current empirical research. *Human Resource Management Review*, 15(1), pp.69-95.

Hofstede, G., 1980. *Culture's Consequences: Comparing Values, Behaviors, Institutions and Organisations Across Nations*. 2nd ed. Thousand Oakes: Sage.

Hofstede, G., 1980. *Culture's Consequences: International Differences in Work Related Values*. Beverly Hills, CA: Sage.

Hofstede, G., 1996. *Cultures and organisations; software of the mind. Intercultural co-operation and its importance for survival*. Revised ed. McGraw-Hill.

Hofstede, G.H., 2001. *Culture's Consequences: Comparing Values, Behaviors, Institutions and Organizations Across Nations*. London: SAGE Publications.

Hofstede, G.H., 2002. *Exploring Culture: Exercises, Stories and Synthetic Cultures*. New York: Intercultural Press.

Hofstede, G., 2011. Dimensionalizing Cultures: The Hofstede Model in Context. *Psychology and Culture*, 2(1), pp.1-26.

Hofstede, G. & Minkov, M., 2010. Long- versus short-term orientation: New perspectives. *Asia Pacific Business Review*, 16(1), pp.493–504.

Hofstede, G., Neuijen, B., Ohayv, D. & Sanders, G., 1990. Measuring organizational cultures: A qualitative and Quantitative study across twenty cases. *Administrative Science Quarterly*, 35(1), pp.286–316.

Jarvenpaa, S.L., Knoll, K. & Leidner, D.E., 1998. Is anybody out there? Antecedents of trust in global virtual teams. *Journal of Management Information Systems*, 14(4), pp.29-64.

Jarvenpaa, S.L. & Leidner, D.E., 1998. Communication and Trust in Global Virtual Teams. *Journal of Computer Mediated Communication*, 3(4).

Jarvenpaa, S.L. & Leidner, D.E., 1999. Communication and trust in global virtual teams. *Organization Science* , 10(6), pp.791-815.

Johnson, J.J., 1999. *A field study of partially distributed group support*. Hawaii: Proceedings of the 32nd Hawaii International Conference on System Sciences.

Jones, , Oyung, & Pace, , 2005. *Working Virtually: Challenges of Virtual Teams*. Hershey: Idea Group Inc (IGI).

Katzenbach, J.R. & Smith, D.K., 1999. *The Wisdom of Teams: Creating the High-Performance Organization*. 2nd ed. New York: HarperCollins.

Kayworth, T. & Dorthy, L., 2000. The Global Virtual Manager: A Perspective for Success. *European Management Journal*, 18(2), pp.183-94.

Khosrowpour, M., 1998. *Effective Utilization and Management of Emerging Information Technologies: 1998 Information Resources Management Association, International Conference, Boston, MA, USA, May 17-20, 1998*. Information Resources Management Association. International Conference ed. New York: Idea Group Inc (IGI).

Khosrowpour, M., 2001. *Managing Information Technology in a Global Economy*. Hershey: Idea Group Inc (IGI).

Khosrowpour, M., 2006. *Emerging Trends and Challenges in Information Technology Management: 2006 Information Resources Management Association International Conference, Washington, DC, USA, May 21-24, 2006, Volume 1*. Idea Group Inc (IGI).

Klitmøller , & Lauring, , 2013. When global virtual teams share knowledge: Media richness, cultural difference and language commonality. *Journal of World Business 48 (2013) 398–406*, 48(1), pp.398–406.

Lewkowicz, M., Fon, W. & Anca , D.(., 2008. *MyMisunderstandings in Global Virtual Engineering-Teams: Definitions, Causes, and Guidelines for Knowledge Sharing and Interaction*. London: Springer.

Lipnack, J. & Stamps, J., 2000. *Virtual Teams: People Working Across Boundaries With Technology*. New York: Wiley.

Luger, E., 2009. *Hofsteede's Cultural Dimensions*. Norderstedt: GRIN Verlag.

Lurey, J.S. & Rasinghani, M.S., 2001. An empirical study of best practices in virtual teams. *Information and Management*, 38(1), pp.523-544.

Lustig, M.W. & Koester, , 2009. *Intercultural Competence: Interpersonal Communication Across Cultures*. 6th ed. Allyn & Bacon, Incorporated.

MacGregor, S.P., 2007. *Higher Creativity for Virtual Teams: Developing Platforms for Co-creation*. New York: Idea Group Inc (IGI).

Magnusson, et al., 2008. Breaking through the cultural clutter: A comparative assessment of multiple cultural and institutional frameworks. *International Marketing Review*, 25(2), pp.183-201..

Majchrzak, A. et al., 2000. Technology adaptation: the case of a computer-supported inter-organizational virtual team. *MIS Quarterly*, 24(4), pp.569-600.

Mäkilouko, M., 2004. Coping with multi-cultural projects: the leadership styles of finnish project managers 22 (2004) 387–. *International Journal of Project Management*, 22(1), pp.387-96.

Mazneyski, L.M. & Chudoba, K.M., 2000. Bridging space over time: global virtual team dynamics and effectiveness. *Organization Science*, 11(5), pp.473-92.

Montoya-Wreiss, M.M., Massey, A.P. & Song, M., 2001. Getting it together: temporal coordination and conflict management in global virtual teams. *Academy of Management Journal*, 44(6), pp.1251-1262.

Moodian, M.A., 2007. *An Analysis of Intercultural Competence Levels of Organizational Leadership Doctoral Students*. An Arbor: Pepperdine University.

Moodian, M.A., 2008. *Contemporary Leadership and Intercultural Competence: Exploring the Cross-Cultural Dynamics Within Organizations*. London: SAGE Publications.

Mowshowitz, A., 1997. Virtual organisation. *Communications of the ACM*, 40(9), pp.30-37.

Nataatmadja, I. & Dyson, L.E., 2006. *ICT and Its Impact on Managing Global*. Sydney: University of Technology, Sydney, Australia.

Neelankavil, R.A., 2004. *Basics of International Business*. New York: M.E. Sharpe.

Nemiro, J.E., 1998. *Creativity in Virtual Teams*. California: Claremont Graduate University.

Nemiro, , Beyerlein, M.M., Bradley, & Beyerlein, , 2008. *The Handbook of High Performance Virtual Teams: A Toolkit for Collaborating Across Boundaries*. New York: John Wiley & Sons.

Pauleen, D., 2004. *Virtual Teams: Projects, Protocols and Processes*. Hershey: Idea Group Inc (IGI).

Peters, L.M. & Manz, C.C., 2007. Identifying antecedents of virtual team collaboration. *Team Performance Management, 13: 117-129*, 13(1), pp.117-29.

Piekkari, R. & Tietze, S., 2011. A world of languages: Implications for international management research and practice. *Journal of World Business*, 46(1), pp.267–69.

Piepenburg, K., 2011. *Critical analysis of Hofstede's model of cultural dimensions: To what extent are his findings reliable, valid and applicable to organisations in the 21st century?* Norderstedt: GRIN Verlag.

Pinjani, P., 2007. *Diversity in Global Virtual Teams: A Partnership Development Perspective*. Ann Arbor: ProQuest.

Powell, A., Piccoli, C. & Ives, B., 2004. Virtual teams : a review of current literature and directions for future research. *The Data base for Advances in Information Systems*, 35(1), pp.6-36.

Puffer, S.M., 2004. *International Management: Insights from Fiction and Practice*. M.E. Sharpe.

Rosenhauer, S., 2008. *Cross-Cultural Business Communication: Intercultural competence as a universal interculture*. Berlin: Diplomarbeiten Agentur.

Rottig, , Reus, T.H. & Tarba, S.Y., 2013. The Impact of Culture on Mergers and Acquisitions: A Third of a Century of Research. In C.L. Cooper, ed. *Advances in Mergers and Acquisitions*. 12th ed. Sydney: Emerald Group Publishing Limited. pp.135-72.

Schimmack, U., Oishi, S. & Diener, E., 2005. Individualism: A valid and important dimension of cultural differences between nations. *Personality and Social Psychology Review*, 9(1), pp.17-31.

Schmidt, W.V., 2007. *Communicating Globally: Intercultural Communication and International Business*. London: SAGE.

Sembdner., S., 2011. *Success Factors of Virtual Teams in the Conflict of Cross-Cultural Team Structures*. Hamburg: Diplomica Verlag.

Settle-Murphy, N.M., 2013. *Leading Effective Virtual Teams: Overcoming Time and Distance to Achieve Exceptional Results*. Boca Raton: CRC Press.

Shachal, P., 2008. Cultural diversity and information and communication technology impacts on global virtual teams: An exploratory study. Information and Management. *Information and Management*, 45(2), pp.131-42.

Stahl, G., Maznevski, M.L., Voght, A. & Jonsen, K., 2010. Unraveling the effects of cultural diversity in teams: A meta-analysis of research in multicultural work groups. *Journal of International Business Studies*, 41(1), pp.690–709.

Stewart, T.A., 1994. Managing in a wired company. *Fortune*, 130(1), pp.44-56.

Steyaert, C., Ostendorp, A. & Gaibrois, C., 2011. Multilingual organizations as 'linguascapes': Negotiating the position of English through discursive practices. *Journal of World Business*, 46(1), pp.270–78.

Suchan, J. & Greg, H., 2001. The Communication Characteristics of Virtual Teams: A Case Study. *IEEE Transactions on Professional Communication*, 44(3), p.174.

Taras, V., Kirkman, B. & Steel, P., 2010. Examining the impact of culture's consequences: A threedecade, multilevel, meta-analytic review of Hofstede's cultural value dimensions. *Journal of Applied Psychology*, 95(1), pp.405-39.

Terpstra, V. & David, K., 1991. *The Cultural Environment of International Business*. Stamford: South-Western Thomson Learning.

Thomas, D.C., 2008. *Cross-Cultural Management: Essential Concepts*. London: SAGE.

Tomovic, C.L., 2011. *Impact of Product Lifecycle Management on Virtual Team Development and Productivity*. Purdue Univeristy.

Vinaja, R., 2004. *Major Challenges in Multi-Cultural Virtual Teams*. University of Texas-Pan American.

Wei-hsin, Y., 2005. Changes in women's postmarital employment in Japan and Taiwan. *Demography*, 42(1), pp.693–717.

Weisinger, J.Y. & Salipante, P.F., 2000. Cultural knowing as practicing: Extending our conceptions of culture. *Journal of Management Inquiry, 9: 376–390.*, 9(1), pp.376–90.

Welch, D.E. & Welch, L.S., 2008. The importance of language in international knowledge transfer. *Mangement International Review*, 48(1), pp.339–60.

Young, P.J., 2001. Relationship building and the use of ICT in boundary-crossing virtual teams: a facilitator's perspective. *Journal of Information Technology*, 16(4), p.205.

Zayani, F.A., 2008. *The Impact of Transformational Leadership on the Success of Global Virtual Teams: An Investigation Based on the Multifactor Leadership Questionnaire*. Ann Arbor: ProQuest.

Zenun, M.M.N., Loureiro, G. & Araujo, C.S., 2007. The Effects of Teams' Co-location on Project Performance. In G. Loureiro & R. Curran, eds. *Complex Systems Concurrent Engineering- Collaboration, Technology Innovation and Sus tainability*. London: Springer.

Zofi, Y., 2011. *A Manager's Guide to Virtual Teams*. New York: AMACOM Div American Mgmt Assn.